R. L. Stine

My Favorite Writer

Neil Purslow

WEIGL PUBLISHERS INC.

Published by Weigl Publishers Inc.
350 5th Avenue, Suite 3304, PMB 6G
New York, NY 10118-0069

Web site: www.weigl.com

Library of Congress Cataloging-in-Publication Data

Purslow, Neil.
  R.L. Stine / Neil Purslow.
      p. cm. -- (My favorite writer)
  Includes index.
  ISBN 1-59036-486-4 (library binding : alk. paper) -- ISBN 1-59036-
487-2 (soft cover : alk. paper)
  1. Stine, R. L.--Juvenile literature. 2. Authors, American--20th century--
Biography--Juvenile literature. 3. Children's stories--Authorship--Juvenile
literature. I. Title. II. Series.
  PS3569.T4837Z89 2007
  813'.54--dc22
  [B]

                                           2006015268

Printed in the United States of America
1 2 3 4 5 6 7 8 9 0 09 08 07 06 05

Project Coordinator
Heather C. Hudak

Design
Terry Paulhus

All of the Internet URLs given in the book were valid at the time of
publication. However, due to the dynamic nature of the Internet, some
addresses may have changed, or sites may have ceased to exist since
publication. While the author and publisher regret any inconvenience this
may cause readers, no responsibility for any such changes can be accepted
by either the author or the publisher.

Contents

R. L. Stine

MILESTONES

1943 Born on October 8 in Columbus, Ohio

1961 Enters Ohio State University and becomes "Jovial Bob"

1965 Graduates from college and becomes a teacher

1966 Moves to New York City and begins writing for magazines

1968 Joins Scholastic as a staff writer

1969 Marries Jane Waldhorn

1975 Creates and edits his own **humor** magazine called *Bananas*

1978 Writes his first children's book, *How to Be Funny*

1980 Son, Matthew, is born

1984 Becomes a freelance writer

1986 His first **horror** novel, *Blind Date*, is published

1989 Launches the Fear Street series with publication of *The New Girl*

1992 Releases the Goosebumps series with its first book, *Welcome to Dead House*

2000 Launches a new series, Nightmare Room

When Robert Lawrence Stine was 7 years old, he crept into the attic of his house. He worried that he might meet an attic monster. Luckily, there was no monster. He had hoped to find some mysterious trunks, eerie moose heads, or flying bats. Instead, he found his parents' old clothes. However, there was one small black case on the floor. He wondered what was inside.

Robert (Bob) opened the case and made an amazing discovery. Inside was a portable typewriter. Soon, his mother appeared. She had told Bob the attic was not safe. As punishment, Bob was sent to his room. However, his mother let him take the typewriter. He quickly began typing—with one finger.

Bob is now the best-selling children's author in history. He has sold more than 250 million books in the Goosebumps **series** and more than 80 million books in the Fear Street series. By the mid-1990s, Bob was writing two books a month. In 2000, he launched a new series for 9- to 12-year-olds, called Nightmare Room. He still types with one finger.

Early Childhood

"Time to go to sleep," Bob would say to his brother, Bill, right in the middle of telling a scary story. Bill always wanted to know what happened next. However, Bob would pretend to go to sleep. He liked leaving his brother in suspense.

R obert Lawrence Stine was born in Columbus, Ohio, on October 8, 1943. He grew up in Bexley, Ohio. Bob lived in a three-story house near railroad tracks. His parents worked hard. Bob's father, Lewis, worked for a restaurant supply company. His mother, Anne, stayed home to look after Bob, his younger brother, Bill, and his sister, Pam.

From an early age, Bob loved comic books. His mother would not let him have comic books because she thought they were not well written. Then, Bob realized that he could read *Mad* and all his other favorite magazines at the barber shop. Almost every Saturday morning, Bob would ask his mother for money to get a haircut. After he had finished reading the new magazines, he would get his hair cut and head home.

Columbus is in central Ohio and is home to more than 700,000 people.

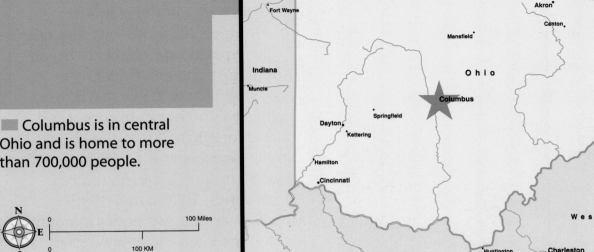

At home, Bob spent most of his time creating his own comic books and magazines. His first magazine was called *The All New Bob Stine Giggle Book*. It was 10 pages long with five pages of jokes and riddles. Bob typed the words using the old typewriter from the attic. He made many magazines using pens, pencils, crayons, tape, paste, scissors, a stapler, and the typewriter. Bob only made one copy of each magazine. They were a great deal of work. He would give the magazines to his friends to read.

Bob and Bill shared a bedroom when they were children. They would lie in bed and look at the shadows on the walls and ceiling. Then they took turns telling stories about ghosts, haunted houses, bats, werewolves, and mummies. The brothers tried to frighten each other.

Columbus lies along the shores of the Scioto and Olentangy rivers. It was named the capital of Ohio in 1816.

Growing Up

From an early age, Bob liked scary things. One of his earliest memories is that of a voice from the popular radio show *Suspense*. Each episode of *Suspense* told a different scary story. He would listen to the show until he became too frightened. Then he would turn off the radio. He would wait a few minutes to build up his courage. Then he would turn on the radio again.

Bob also liked to read **science fiction**. He especially enjoyed stories written by Isaac Asimov, Ray Bradbury, and Robert Sheckley. As Bob grew older, he read everything from fairy tales to myths and legends. He had very little interest in reading about real people and places.

For many years, Bob used an old typewriter to write his stories.

Every Sunday, Bob and Bill would head down to the local theater to see a horror movie. They enjoyed the 1950s thrillers *It Came from Beneath the Sea, Night of the Living Dead,* and *The Creature from the Black Lagoon.* His favorite movies featured monsters destroying major cities.

When Bob was 13 years old, he began to prepare for his **bar mitzvah**. His parents wanted to buy him a special gift. Bob asked for a new typewriter. They bought him a good quality typewriter that he used for many years.

Inspired to Write

Bob believes that the first step to being a writer is to read often. Reading books by many authors helps you learn different ways of saying things and describing people, **settings**, and events. You will also increase your **vocabulary**.

The monster from *The Creature from the Black Lagoon* gave Bob thrills and chills.

As a teenager, Bob continued to create and publish his own magazines, such as *HAH, for Maniacs Only!* It **spoofed** many popular television shows. In one case, a popular show called *The 64-Thousand-Dollar Question* became *The 64-Thousand-Dollar Answer*. In another, *Dragnet* became *Dragnut*. This was followed by *Tales to Drive You Batty* and *Whammy*. Next came *Bozos on Patrol, Stine's Line,* and *BARF*. In these last three creations, Bob attached funny **captions** to pictures he cut out of magazines.

During his junior and senior high school years, Bob continued to watch scary movies and read frightening books. However, he wanted to make a career out of writing funny stories. Bob was accepted to Ohio State University in 1961. He became the **editor** of the university's humor magazine, *Sundial*, in his second year at the college.

"My job is to make kids laugh and give them the creeps!"
Bob Stine

Harry Morgan played Officer Bill Gannon on television's *Dragnet*. Bob would later spoof the show in his own writings.

Sundial made fun of living at college. Bob became known as Jovial Bob because of his humor and **practical jokes**. The magazine did very well under Jovial Bob's leadership. It became the number one college magazine in the United States in 1965.

Ray Bradbury is mainly known for writing science fiction short stories. He is one of Bob's favorite writers.

Favorite Authors

Bob was a fan of science fiction early in life. He especially liked the stories written by Isaac Asimov and Ray Bradbury. Bradbury's book *Something Wicked This Way Comes* is Bob's favorite scary book. It tells the story of two 13-year-old boys who visit a carnival that comes to town with a mysterious ringmaster. Bob is also fond of Robert Sheckley's *Mindswap*. In this story, the mind of a human is swapped with an alien's mind for two weeks. Bob also enjoyed reading all of Edgar Allan Poe's scary stories.

Learning the Craft

When Bob graduated from college, he became a substitute teacher. He wrote that being a substitute teacher was "scarier than the scariest walk down Fear Street!" While teaching, Bob wrote a two-minute comedy for radio. It was called *Captain Anything*. He had two popular radio hosts from Columbus, Ohio, provide the voices. Then he sent a recording sample to radio stations across the United States. No one would air his show.

By 1966, Bob had saved enough money to move to New York City. One of his first jobs was working for the editor of six teenage fan magazines. Bob wrote a number of interviews with big stars of the 1960s, including the Beatles, Tom Jones, the Rolling Stones, and the Jacksons. However, he never met any of these stars. All of the interviews were imaginary. At the same time, Bob wrote his first horror stories. He authored "Bony Fingers from the Grave," "Trapped in the Vampire's Web of Icy Death," and "It Takes Two for Terror" for a new magazine. However, the magazine was shut down before his stories could be published.

Bob loved listening to scary programs on the radio when he was a child.

After working for a magazine called *Soft Drink Industry*, Bob became a **staff writer** for Junior Scholastic magazines. During his time at Scholastic, Bob met Jane Waldhorn. They married in 1969 and had one son, Matthew.

In 1975, Bob was asked to start a humor magazine for teenagers. It was called *Bananas*. *Bananas* offered such articles as "How to Turn Your Uncle into a Coffee Table," "How to Tell If You Are an Alien from Outer Space," and "How to Turn Your Poems into Dog Food." Bob was living his dream of writing humor.

Inspired to Write

Most writers create their stories first and then come up with the titles. However, Bob starts out with a really good title. Then he writes the story. He thinks it is important for writers to understand how they get their ideas so that they can keep coming up with new ideas.

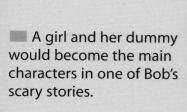 A girl and her dummy would become the main characters in one of Bob's scary stories.

Getting Published

> *"Someone once called me the 'Jekyll and Hyde of children's books.' I guess that's about right. I wrote about 30 or 40 joke books and humor books before I slipped into my 'horror' identity. These days, I'm scary all the time."*
> **Bob Stine**

One day, Bob's phone rang. It was an editor from E.P. Dutton, a publisher of children's books. The editor enjoyed reading *Bananas* and thought it was funny. She wanted Bob to write a funny children's book. After many weeks of thinking about ideas, he decided on the title *How to Be Funny*. It would be a very silly guidebook to help children be funny. The book was published in 1978. This was Bob's first book.

In 1984, *Bananas* went out of business. Bob then became a full-time **freelance writer**. He wrote joke books, including *101 Silly Monster Jokes, Sick of Being Sick,* and *Bored of Being Bored*. He also wrote GI Joe action stories, Indiana Jones novels, junior James Bond books, and mystery books. *Madballs* was a series of books Bob wrote about rubber balls with faces. "Somebody's got to write that stuff," he has said of his books.

The Publishing Process

Publishing companies receive hundreds of **manuscripts** from authors each year. Only a few manuscripts become books. Publishers must be sure that a manuscript will sell many copies. As a result, publishers reject most of the manuscripts they receive.

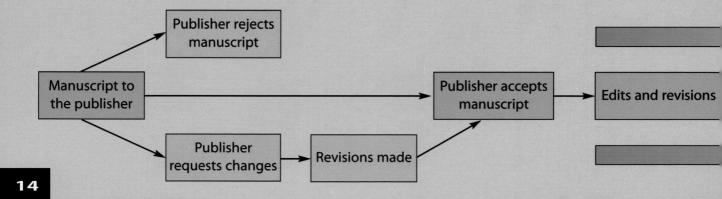

Bob was then asked to become the lead writer of a preschool children's television program. It was called *Eureeka's Castle*. After his first year, the show won an Ace Award for best children's show on cable television.

In 1986, Bob had lunch with a publisher. She asked Bob if he had ever thought about writing horror novels for teenagers. Bob had always liked horror but had never thought of writing these types of books. He began by researching similar novels.

However, Bob wanted his book to be funnier and less **gory** than others. He also wanted to write for an 8- to 12-year-old audience. After about five months, the horror novel *Blind Date* was finished. It was published in 1986. Bob decided to use the name R. L. Stine for his horror books since it was scarier than Jovial Bob.

Inspired to Write

Like many writers, Bob writes about things he remembers from the past. In his books, Bob has used many ideas from the scary stories he and his brother told each other when they were young.

Once a manuscript has been accepted, it goes through many stages before it is published. Often, authors change their work to follow an editor's suggestions. Once the book is published, some authors receive royalties. This is money based on book sales.

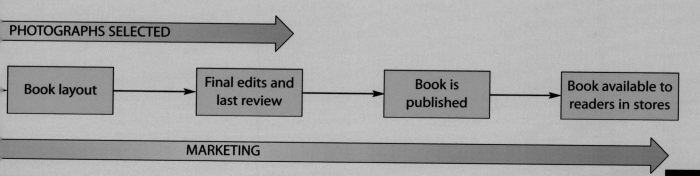

PHOTOGRAPHS SELECTED →

Book layout → Final edits and last review → Book is published → Book available to readers in stores

MARKETING →

Writer Today

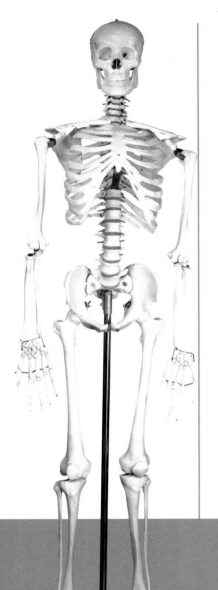

Blind Date was a **bestseller**. The publisher asked Bob to write another horror book. This one was called *Twisted*, which was soon followed by *The Baby-sitter*. All were bestsellers. Bob had found something that young readers really liked—to be scared.

Bob decided to write a series of books in the horror **genre**. He needed to come up with a name for the series. Fear Street popped into his head. These books would be written for 9- to 14-year-olds. The first book was *The New Girl*. It was published in 1989. This was followed by *The Surprise Party* and *The Overnight*.

Then someone suggested to Bob that he try writing scary books for younger children. Again, he needed to come up with a name for the series. One day, while looking through the television listings, he saw an advertisement for "Goosebumps Week." He decided the name for his new series would be Goosebumps.

Goosebumps was launched in 1992 with *Welcome to Dead House*. It was an instant success. Millions of copies were sold.

By the mid-1990s, he was writing an average of two books each month. The main difference between the two series is that children do not die in the Goosebumps stories. In Fear Street, many teens can perish. Bob spends about 6 days a week working on his scary books.

Bob's stories may include creepy creatures, such as ghosts or skeletons, but he does not want to give his readers nightmares.

Bob's wife and four other editors review each story. Like many writers, Bob dislikes revising his stories. "I'm always eager to get on to the next story. I hate to go back and fix up an old story," he has said. Bob has sold more than 250 million books in the Goosebumps series, and more than 80 million books in the Fear Street series.

In 2000, Bob launched another series called Nightmare Room. This series also has an interactive website where readers can create their own scary stories.

Bob's Goosebumps series has been made into a television show.

Popular Books

Bob has written many stories. He has authored more than 80 books in the Goosebumps series. Following are some of his favorite books.

Night of the Living Dummy

In *Night of the Living Dummy*, Lindy finds a ventriloquist's dummy and names it Slappy. Slappy is quite ugly, but he is still a lot of fun. Lindy is having a great time learning to make Slappy move and talk. However, Lindy's sister, Kris, is jealous of the attention Lindy and her dummy are getting. Kris decides to get her own dummy. Soon, weird things begin to happen.

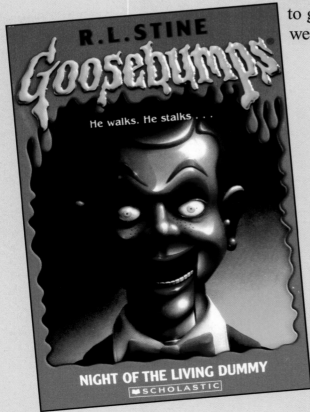

R.L. STINE

Goosebumps

He walks. He stalks . . .

NIGHT OF THE LIVING DUMMY

SCHOLASTIC

Don't Forget Me

Danielle, her parents, and younger brother, Peter, have just moved into a new home. Danielle finds her brother annoying and sometimes wishes she was an only child. One night, when her parents are not at home, Danielle hears voices calling from the basement. Her dream to be an only child becomes a nightmare.

The Haunted Mask

In *The Haunted Mask*, Steve Boswell wants to have the scariest costume on the block. He buys a mask that looks like a creepy old man with stringy hair, a wrinkled face, and spiders crawling out of his ears. But Steve finds it may be more than a mask. He begins feeling old, tired, and evil.

Stay Out of the Basement

Dr. Brewer is testing plants in his basement. He says his work is harmless. However, his children are worried. Margaret and Casey Brewer become concerned when they see some of the plants. They also begin to notice that their father is becoming more like his plants. It is up to Margaret and Casey to discover whether their father's work really is safe.

Hide and Shriek

Do you believe in ghosts? Randy Clay has just moved to Fear Street in a strange town called Shadyside. Every year, the town celebrates the birthday of a boy named Pete, who died years ago. The children in town play a game of "hide and shriek" with Pete's ghost in the woods at night. When Pete tags someone, he lives in their body for the next year. As the game begins this year, Randy hears footsteps behind her and feels breathing on her neck. She runs to the cemetery to avoid being tagged. Is she fast enough?

Switched

In *Switched*, Nicole always thought her friend Lucy's life was so much better than her own. She had cooler parents and a cuter boyfriend. Next to Lucy, Nicole felt badly about herself. So when Lucy asked if she wanted to switch bodies, Nicole thought it sounded like a fun idea. At least it would be good for a laugh. What she did not realize is that the plan to trade bodies would actually work—or that Lucy's life might not be so terrific after all.

It turns out that Lucy has some problems, and she is about to take revenge—using Nicole's body.

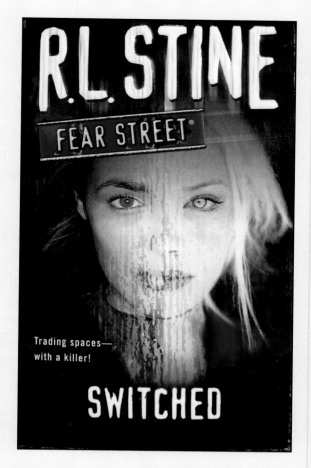

Trading spaces— with a killer!

SWITCHED

The Face

Martha was in a horrible accident, and she cannot remember what happened to her. Her friends will not talk about it. They say she will remember in time. However, someone wants her to remember immediately. Martha draws this person's face over and over. It is the face of a dead boy she does not know. Martha finds she cannot control her hand as she draws the boy's face, and she cannot remember how he died. She is determined to find the answer.

AWARDS

Goosebumps: *Deep Trouble II*

1998 Named Favorite Book at Nickelodeon's Kids' Choice Awards

Nightmare Room: *Locker 13*

2000 Named Best Horror/Mystery Book at *Disney Adventures*' Kids' Choice Awards

Goosebumps series

2000 Second on National Education Association list of kids' favorite books

Creative Writing Tips

The process for writing **fiction** is different for each author. There is no best way—only what works well for the writer. Each writer has to find his or her own style. Here are some things to think about as you write.

Use Your Past Experiences for Ideas

Use things that you remember from the past to help you create ideas for your stories. Things that scared Bob in the past often became ideas he used in his stories. For instance, many children believe a monster lives in the basement. Bob had the same fear. He used this experience to help him write the Goosebumps story *I Live in Your Basement*.

Stretch Your Imagination

Once you have an idea, fire up your imagination. You can expand that simple idea to create a story plot or chapter. Try putting ordinary characters into situations that they would not normally experience. Your story's main character might become involved in a great deal of trouble. Add more characters to the mix. Have other characters dream up ways to help your main character solve his or her problem.

Like Bob, children can use their imagination to write exciting stories.

Organize Your Thoughts and Ideas

Once you have a plot and some ideas, they need to be organized. Bob uses an **outline** for his stories. His outline contains everything that happens in the book. It even includes the chapter endings. Once the outline is complete, he begins writing. The outline ensures that the story ideas are in the right order. It also ensures that all ideas are included in the story. Bob did not prepare outlines when he first started writing books. He now prepares one for every book he writes.

Practice, Practice, Practice

It takes practice to write a good story. Bob began writing books when he was 12 years old. Since those early years, he has been writing constantly. When he began writing horror stories, Bob read books by other horror authors to learn how they wrote. His first horror book took him nearly five months to complete. Through practice, Bob is now able to complete an outline and write a book in the Fear Street and Goosebumps series in about 10 or 11 days.

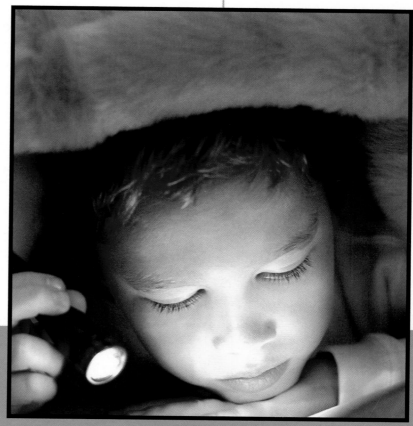

Reading stories written by others can help you become a better writer.

Writing a Biography Review

A biography is an account of an individual's life that is written by another person. Some people's lives are very interesting. In school, you may be asked to write a biography review. The first thing to do when writing a biography review is to decide whom you would like to learn about. Your school library or community library will have a large selection of biographies from which to choose.

Are you interested in an author, a sports figure, an inventor, a movie star, or a president? Finding the right book is your first task. Whether you choose to write your review on a biography of R.L. Stine or another person, the task will be similar.

Begin your review by writing the title of the book, the author, and the person featured in the book. Then, start writing about the main events in the person's life. Include such things as where the person grew up and what his or her childhood was like. You will want to add details about the person's adult life, such as whether he or she married or had children. Next, write about what you think makes this person special. What kinds of experiences influenced this individual? For instance, did he or she grow up in unusual circumstances? Was the person determined to accomplish a goal? Include any details that surprised you.

A concept web is a useful research tool. Use the concept web on the right to begin researching your biography review.

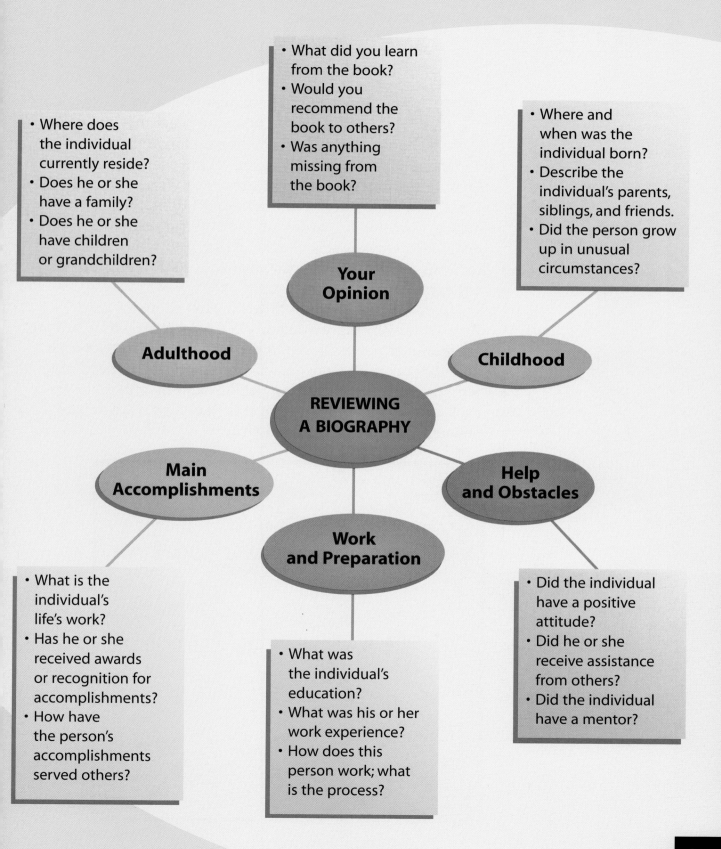

• Where does the individual currently reside?
• Does he or she have a family?
• Does he or she have children or grandchildren?

• What did you learn from the book?
• Would you recommend the book to others?
• Was anything missing from the book?

• Where and when was the individual born?
• Describe the individual's parents, siblings, and friends.
• Did the person grow up in unusual circumstances?

Your Opinion

Adulthood

Childhood

REVIEWING A BIOGRAPHY

Main Accomplishments

Help and Obstacles

Work and Preparation

• What is the individual's life's work?
• Has he or she received awards or recognition for accomplishments?
• How have the person's accomplishments served others?

• What was the individual's education?
• What was his or her work experience?
• How does this person work; what is the process?

• Did the individual have a positive attitude?
• Did he or she receive assistance from others?
• Did the individual have a mentor?

Fan Information

When Bob writes a book, his goal is to scare readers. However, he is sad when he hears that one of his books has given a child a nightmare.

Bob receives thousands of fan letters each week. His favorite fan letter came from a boy who wrote, "Dear R. L. Stine, I've read 40 of your books and I think they're really boring." Despite his boredom, the boy had read 40 of Bob's books. Bob makes sure that everyone who writes to him receives a reply. At one time, he had a staff of five people answering his fan mail.

To encourage children to write, Bob sponsors the R. L. Stine Writing Workshops in Columbus's public schools. Professional writers come to the schools for 2 weeks each year to work with students who are interested in becoming writers. Bob also visits many children in their classrooms each year. He tells them what it is like to be a writer and encourages them to read and write.

Bob receives many fan letters. One time, the letter carrier left Bob a large canvas mailbag full of letters near the door of his apartment.

Bob meets his fans at book festivals, such as the *Los Angeles Times* Festival of Books.

WEB LINKS

Goosebumps home page
www.scholastic.com/goosebumps

This website offers information about the Goosebumps series. It includes a description for every book in the series, plus games, DVDs, an interview with Bob, and more.

Nightmare Room
www.thenightmareroom.com

This interactive site allows readers to make choices online to create their own personal nightmares.

Quiz

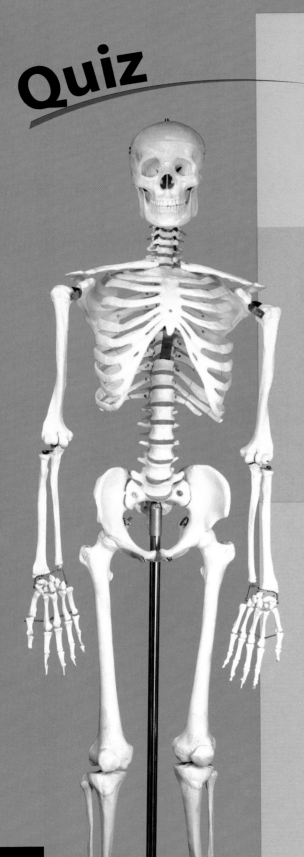

Q: When and where was Bob Stine born?

A: October 8, 1943, in Columbus, Ohio

Q: When Bob was younger, where did he go every Saturday morning to read comic books and magazines?

A: The barber shop

Q: When Bob went to college, he wrote and edited for an on-campus humor magazine. What was its name?

A: Sundial

4

Q: What humor magazine did Bob start when he was with Scholastic?

A: *Bananas*

5

Q: Who did Bob marry?

A: *Jane Waldhorn*

6

Q: Bob became the lead writer for which TV show?

A: *Eureeka's Castle*

7

Q: What is the name of Bob's brother?

A: *Bill*

8

Q: What was the name of Bob's first horror book?

A: *Blind Date*

9

Q: What is the name of the series Bob launched in 2000?

A: *Nightmare Room*

10

Q: What is the name of Bob's most successful series?

A: *Goosebumps*

Writing Terms

This glossary will introduce you to some of the main terms in the field of writing. Understanding these common writing terms will allow you to discuss your ideas about books and writing with others.

action: the moving events of a work of fiction

antagonist: the person in the story who opposes the main character

autobiography: a history of a person's life written by that person

biography: a written account of another person's life

character: a person in a story, poem, or play

climax: the most exciting moment or turning point in a story

episode: a short piece of action, or scene, in a story

fiction: stories about characters and events that are not real

foreshadow: hinting at something that is going to happen later in the book

imagery: a written description of a thing or idea that brings an image to mind

narrator: the speaker of the story who relates the events

nonfiction: writing that deals with real people and events

novel: published writing of considerable length that portrays characters within a story

plot: the order of events in a work of fiction

protagonist: the leading character of a story; often a likable character

resolution: the end of the story, when the conflict is settled

scene: a single episode in a story

setting: the place and time in which a work of fiction occurs

theme: an idea that runs throughout a work of fiction

Glossary

bar mitzvah: a religious ceremony in which a Jewish boy becomes an adult

bestseller: a book that has extremely high sales

captions: the words that describe pictures in a book, magazine, or newspaper

editor: someone who prepares a manuscript for publication

fiction: characters and events that are not real

freelance writer: a writer who works on his or her own, not as an employee at a company

genre: a specific type or kind of literature

gory: violent or bloody

horror: a feeling of great fear that makes a person shudder

humor: something that is funny or amusing

manuscripts: drafts of a story before it is published

outline: a summary of everything that happens in a book

practical jokes: tricks played on someone, especially those intended to embarrass the person

science fiction: movies, stories, and books that are fantastic and that make use of scientific devices, space travel, robots, and other things that are real or imagined

series: a set of similar things

settings: the places where events in a stories happen

spoofed: poked fun at

staff writer: a writer who works as an employee

vocabulary: all the words of a language

Index

Photo Credits

Every reasonable effort has been made to trace ownership and to obtain permission to reprint copyright material. The publishers would be pleased to have any errors or omiss brought to their attention so that they may be corrected in subsequent printings.

Dan Nelken Studio: cover, page 1.